Biscuit's Birthday

story by ALYSSA SATIN CAPUCILLI
pictures by PAT SCHORIES

HarperFestival®
A Division of HarperCollinsPublishers

"Wake up, sleepy Biscuit!" said the little girl.
"Do you know what day it is?"
Woof!

"Today is a very special day.
It's your birthday!"

Woof! Woof!

"Follow me, Biscuit," said the little girl.
"I have something special planned just for you."

"Surprise, Biscuit! Puddles and Daisy are here for your birthday party!"

Bow wow!
Meow!

"Come along, everybody.
It's time to play some
birthday games."

Woof, woof!
Bow wow!
Meow!

"Silly Biscuit!" called the little girl.
"Be careful with those balloons."

"Oh, no," said the little girl. "There go the balloons!"
Woof!

"Oh, Biscuit!" The little girl laughed. "You may be a year older, but you will always be my silly little puppy."

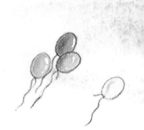

"Now it's time for birthday treats,"
said the little girl.
"Make a wish, Biscuit."

Woof!

"Funny puppy! You want to open your birthday presents!"

"Look, Biscuit! A new collar, a new bone, and best of all . . ."

Woof, woof!

"A new box of biscuits!
Happy birthday, Biscuit!"

Woof!

Word Search

Do you see these words? Circle each one you find.
Be sure to look across and down.

HAPPY   BIRTHDAY   PARTY   CAKE   PRESENT   TOY

To see the answers, turn to the last page.

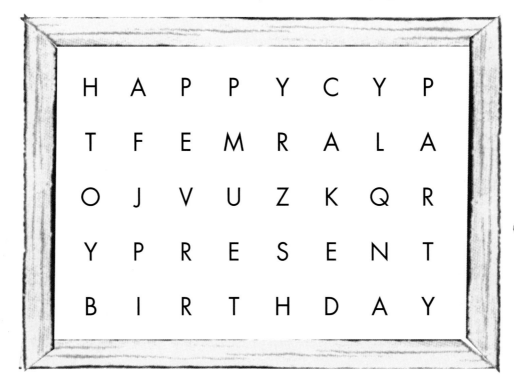

H	A	P	P	Y	C	Y	P
T	F	E	M	R	A	L	A
O	J	V	U	Z	K	Q	R
Y	P	R	E	S	E	N	T
B	I	R	T	H	D	A	Y

Birthday Maze

Help Biscuit find his birthday treat!

Start here.

Happy birthday, Biscuit!

Where's Biscuit?

Connect the dots from one to thirty-four to see what Biscuit is up to.

Color by Numbers with Biscuit!

Following the color key below, use crayons to color in the picture of Biscuit and the little girl.

1=red   3=yellow   5=purple
2=blue   4=green   6=peach

Mixed-up Words

These words are all mixed-up! Can you fix them?
Hint—they're all in the story.

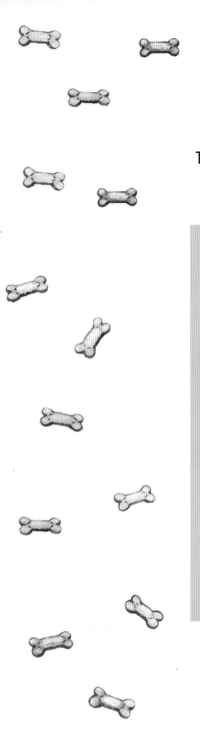

PYPPU

OLLANOB

SEPTERN

PRYTA

To see the answers, turn to the last page.

Birthday Treats

What will Biscuit and his friends eat at his party?
Circle the pictures of their favorite foods.

Answers

Word Search

Birthday Maze

Mixed-up Words

PUPPY

BALLOON

PRESENT

PARTY

Meet Biscuit!

Meet Biscuit!

story by ALYSSA SATIN CAPUCILLI
pictures by PAT SCHORIES

HarperFestival®
A Division of HarperCollins*Publishers*

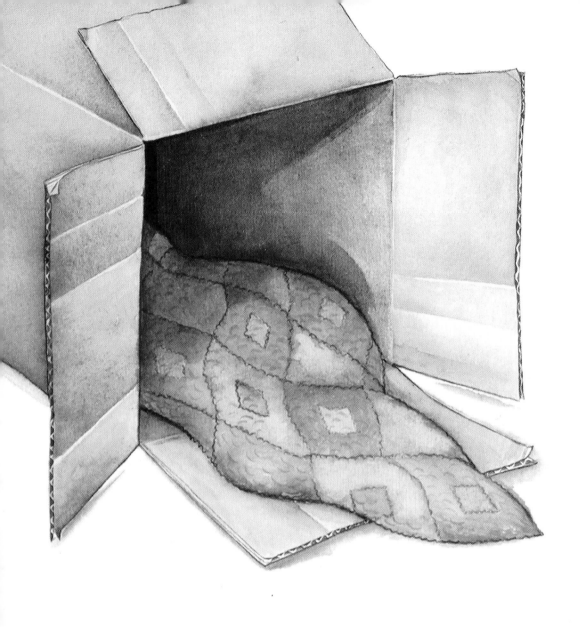

"Here we are, puppy," said the little girl.
"Welcome to your new home!"
Woof, woof!

"The first thing we must do
is find a name for you.
Let's see. You are small and yellow . . ."

Woof, woof!

"Silly puppy! Come back here!"

Woof!

"You found your bed,
and your bone,
and your biscuits."

Woof, woof!

"But no biscuits yet," said the little girl.
"First we must find a name for you!"

"Let's see. You are small and yellow . . .
Wait, little puppy! Where are you going now?"

Woof, woof!

"You found your ball and your toys."
Woof!

"And you found your biscuits again!"
Woof, woof!

"See?" said the little girl.
"You have everything a puppy could need.
Everything except a name!"
Woof, woof!

"Now, what is your name going to be?"
Woof!
"Silly puppy! How did you get those biscuits?"
Woof, woof!

"Oh, no! Come back here with those biscuits!"
Woof, woof, woof, woof!

"That's it!" the little girl cried. "Biscuit!"
Woof!
"Biscuit is the perfect name for you!"
Woof, woof!

"Hello, Biscuit!
You found a name all by yourself!"

Woof!

Draw a Puppy

What would *your* new puppy look like? Draw a picture here!

Connect the Dots

Who is underneath the blanket?
Starting with number 1, connect the dots in sequence to find out.

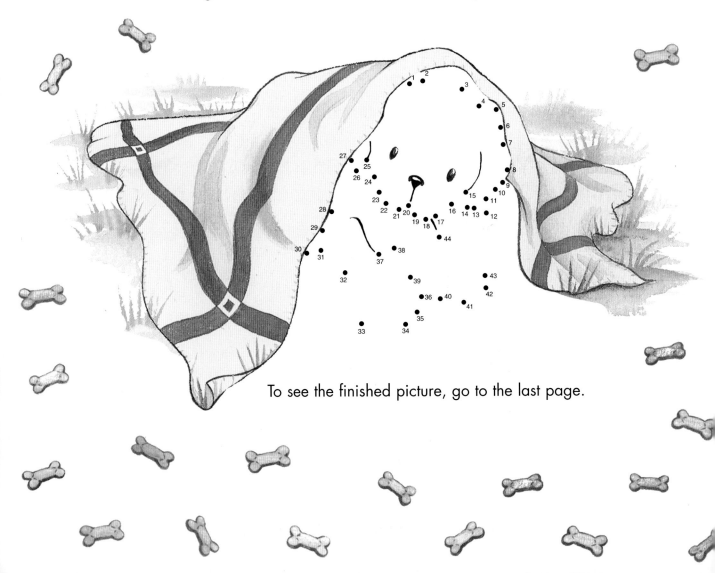

To see the finished picture, go to the last page.

Mixed-up Words

These words are all mixed-up! Can you fix them?
Here's a hint—they're all in the story!

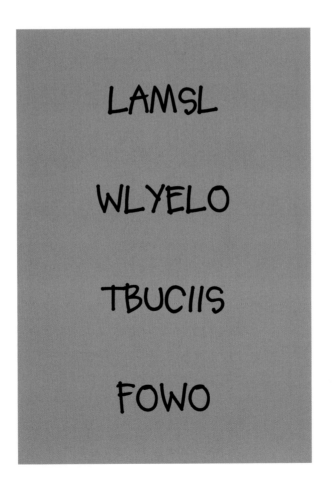

LAMSL

WLYELO

TBUCIIS

FOWO

To see the answers, turn to the last page.

Maze

Help Biscuit get to his favorite treats!

To see the answer, turn to the last page.

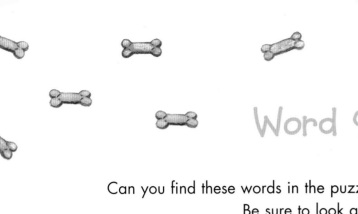

Word Search

Can you find these words in the puzzle below? Circle each one you find.
Be sure to look across and down!

PUPPY   BED   BONE   BALL   TOYS

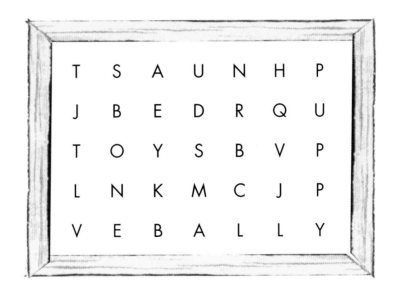

T	S	A	U	N	H	P
J	B	E	D	R	Q	U
T	O	Y	S	B	V	P
L	N	K	M	C	J	P
V	E	B	A	L	L	Y

To see the answers, go to the last page.

Answers

Connect the Dots

Mixed-up Words

SMALL, YELLOW, BISCUIT, WOOF

Maze

Word Search

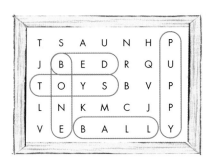

Mind Your Manners, Biscuit!

by Alyssa Satin Capucilli

HarperFestival®
A Division of HarperCollins*Publishers*

"It's a beautiful day
for a walk, Biscuit."
Woof, woof!

"Mom has a list of errands, and we can help.
Let's go!"
Woof!

"We can mail a letter at the post office, Biscuit."
Woof, woof!

"Funny puppy! Come back.
It's not our turn yet."
Woof!

"Here's the pet shop, Biscuit.
You need a new bone and a new ball."
Woof, woof!

"Sit, Biscuit, sit. Mind your manners, silly puppy!
Now Mr. Brown will give you a biscuit.
Thank you, Mr. Brown."
Woof!

"Come along, Biscuit.
It's time to visit the library.
We can return this book and choose
another book to borrow.
We can listen to a story, too."

Woof, woof! Woof, woof!
"Sshhh! Quiet, Biscuit!
That's too loud for inside the library."
Woof!

"The florist is next on Mom's list.
This plant is just right for our garden."
Woof, woof!

"Oh, no, Biscuit. No digging!"
Woof!

"We must help clean up.
That's the way, Biscuit."

"We're almost finished with our errands, Biscuit.
We need bread, eggs, and bananas from the market."
Woof, woof!

"Good puppy!
You can carry a bag, too."
Woof!

"Look, Biscuit!
Our friends are at the ice cream shop!
What shall we have?"
Woof, woof!

"Sweet puppy!
You found a tasty treat to share with Puddles."
Bow wow!
Woof!

"It's time to go home, Biscuit.
Our walk was a lot of fun."
Woof, woof!

"Helping with errands is lots of fun, too,
especially with a sweet puppy like you!"
Woof!

Say hello, Biscuit!
Woof, woof!
Biscuit greets others in his special way.
Draw a circle around the words that we say when
we greet people. Draw a square around the words
we say when it's time to leave.

Hello

Bye

How are you?

Good-bye

I'm pleased to meet you.

It was nice seeing you.

See you soon!

Hi

To see the answer, turn to the last page.

Wait your turn, Biscuit!
Biscuit must learn to be patient.
What treat is there for Biscuit when he waits his turn?
Help Biscuit through the maze to find out.

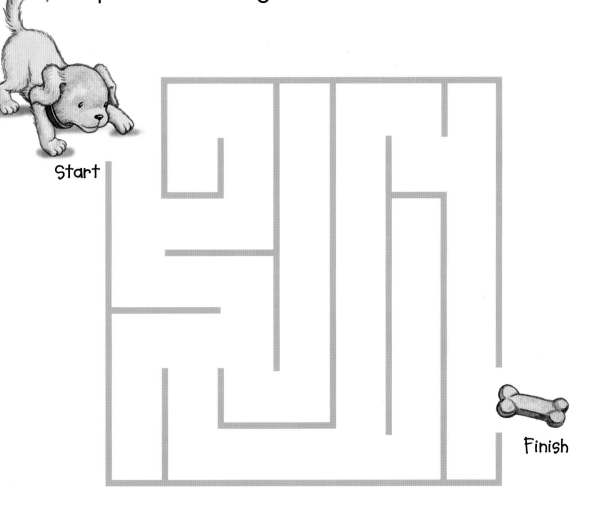

Start

Finish

To see the answer, turn to the last page.

Sometimes we must use voices that are quiet.
Sometimes we can use voices that are loud.
Draw a blue circle around places where we should use a quiet voice, or an inside voice.
Draw a red circle around places we can use a loud voice, or our outside voice.

To see the answer, turn to the last page.

It's nice to share, Biscuit!
Biscuit likes to share a bone
with his friend Puddles.
What do you like to share with your friends?
Draw a picture of things you like to share.

It's fun to help, Biscuit!
Biscuit knows lots of ways to help.
What are some ways that you like to help?

I can help by

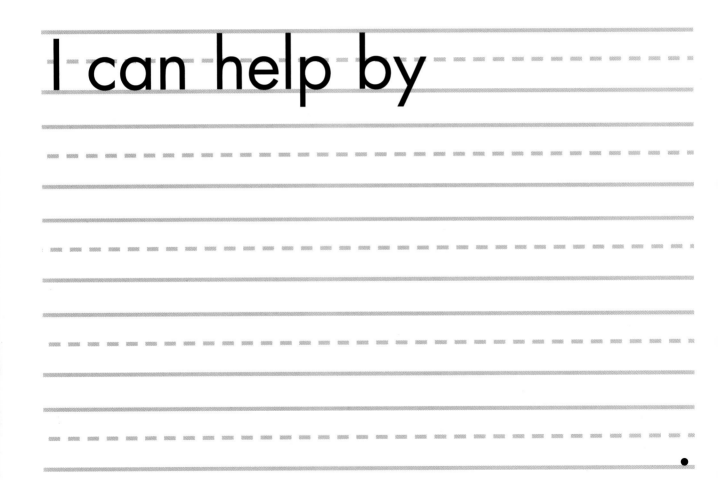

Mind your manners, Biscuit!
Help Biscuit unscramble these letters
to find words that help us to be polite.

spalee

hantk ouy

m'l rrosy

csueex em

ouy'er elcmowe

To see the answer, turn to the last page.

ANSWER KEY

Say hello, Biscuit!

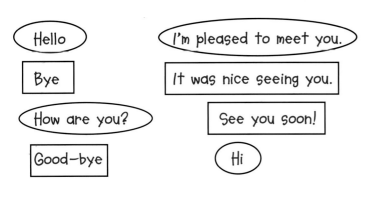

(Hello)

[Bye]

(How are you?)

[Good-bye]

(I'm pleased to meet you.)

[It was nice seeing you.]

[See you soon!]

(Hi)

Quiet in the library, Biscuit!

Wait your turn, Biscuit!

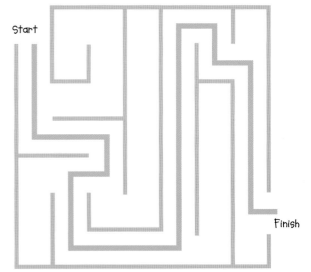

Start

Finish

Mind your manners, Biscuit!

please

thank you

I'm sorry

excuse me

you're welcome

Biscuit's
Show and Share Day

by Alyssa Satin Capucilli
pictures by Mary O'Keefe Young

 HarperFestival®
A Division of HarperCollinsPublishers

"Today is show and share day at school, Biscuit. What shall I bring to show and share with my class?"
Woof, woof!

"Maybe I will bring my favorite teddy bear."
Woof, woof!

"Funny puppy!
You found your favorite blanket."
Woof!

"A seashell would be fun to show and share,
or a picture of the new baby!"
Woof, woof!

"Silly puppy!
It's not time to play ball now.
It's almost time for school."

"Now, let's see. What shall I bring?"
Woof, woof! Woof, woof!

"Oh, no, Biscuit.
How did you get that box of biscuits?"
Woof!

Beep! Beep!
"There's the school bus, Biscuit.
It's time for school!"
Woof, woof!

"Wait, Biscuit. Come back!
Where are you going with my backpack?"
Woof, woof!

"Oh, Biscuit.
You want to go to school today.
You want to be my show and share!"
Woof, woof!

"I can hardly wait for everyone to meet you, Biscuit.
Come along, sweet puppy!
There's my teacher."
Woof, woof!

"Welcome to school, Biscuit.
This is going to be the most special
show and share day of all!"
Woof, woof!

Which Way?
Help Biscuit find his way to school!

To see the answer, turn to the last page.

Snack Time

It's time for a treat!

What does Biscuit like to eat?

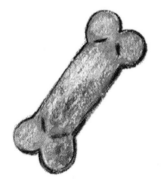

To see the answer, turn to the last page.

Mixed-Up Words

These words are all mixed-up! Can you fix them?
Here's a hint—they're all in the story!

UPPYP

SLACS

OHWS

RHASE

To see the answers, turn to the last page.

Animal Art

It's time for art class!

Can you draw your favorite animal?

Find the Difference

Look closely at these pictures.
Which one is different?

To see the answer, turn to the last page.

Word Search

Can you find these words in the puzzle below?
Circle each one you find.
Be sure to look across and down!

SCHOOL   BISCUIT   BACKPACK   TEACHER   WOOF

B	A	C	K	P	A	C	K
I	J	M	R	W	Q	U	D
S	N	K	J	O	L	E	S
C	S	C	H	O	O	L	M
U	E	B	F	F	N	Y	Z
I	T	E	A	C	H	E	R
T	B	D	G	L	X	P	K

To see the answers, turn to the last page.

Answer Key

Which Way?

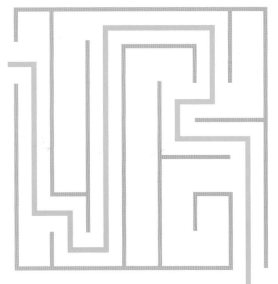

Mixed-Up Words
Puppy, Class, Show, Share

Find the Difference

Snack Time

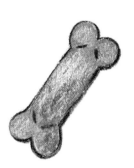

Word Search

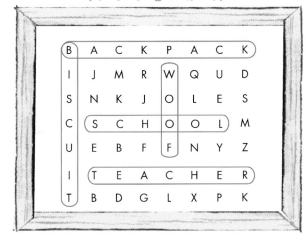

B	A	C	K	P	A	C	K
I	J	M	R	W	Q	U	D
S	N	K	J	O	L	E	S
C	S	C	H	O	O	L	M
U	E	B	F	F	N	Y	Z
I	T	E	A	C	H	E	R
T	B	D	G	L	X	P	K

Biscuit Visits the Doctor

For the wonderful veterinarians
who keep pets healthy . . . everywhere!
—A.S.C

by Alyssa Satin Capucilli

 HarperFestival®
A Division of HarperCollins*Publishers*

Based on the illustration style of Pat Schories
Interior illustrations by Rose Mary Berlin
Biscuit Visits the Doctor
Text copyright © 2008 by Alyssa Satin Capucilli. Illustrations copyright © 2008 by Pat Schories.

Library of Congress catalog card number: 2008924823
ISBN 978-0-06-112843-1
17 18 19 20 SCP 20 19 18

"Come along, Biscuit.
We're going to visit Dr. Green.
It's time for your checkup!"
Woof, woof!

"Dr. Green is a veterinarian, Biscuit.
She cares for many different animals.
Dr. Green makes sure they are all healthy and strong."
Woof, woof!

"There are bunnies and gerbils. . . ."

Squawk! Squawk!
Woof, woof!

"And you found a parrot, Biscuit!"
Woof!

"Here comes Dr. Green."
Woof, woof!

"Are you ready, Biscuit?
It's our turn now."
Woof!

"First, Dr. Green will weigh and measure you, Biscuit.
Let's see how much you've grown!"
Woof, woof!

"Funny puppy! No tugging."
Woof!

"Dr. Green will look at your paws.
She'll listen to your heartbeat, too."
Woof, woof! Woof, woof!

"Shhh! Quiet, Biscuit!"

"Sit, Biscuit, sit.
Dr. Green will check your eyes and your ears."
Woof!

"She can even check your teeth. Open wide, Biscuit!
That's the way!"
Woof, woof!

"You must hold still when
Dr. Green gives you a shot, Biscuit.
She wants you to stay healthy and strong, too.
That wasn't so bad, was it?"
Woof, woof!

"Oh, no, Biscuit!
It's not time to roll over now!"
Woof!
"Silly puppy!"

"You did a great job, Biscuit.
Dr. Green has a special treat just for you."
Woof, woof!

"And you have a special treat for Dr. Green.
It's a big kiss!"
Woof, woof!

"Come along, Biscuit.
It's time to go home."
Woof, woof!
"Wait, Biscuit.

What have you found now?"

Woof, woof!
"Sweet puppy.
There are three little kittens."

Mew! Mew! Mew!
Woof!

"Off we go, Biscuit.
It was fun to visit with our friend Dr. Green."
Woof, woof!
"And meet some new friends, too!"
Woof!